MW01172342

www.yvonnecapehart.org

Published by: YC Publishing
P.O. Box 10462 - Pensacola, FL 32514
ISBN 978-0-9710441-9-7
Printed in the United States of America
For Worldwide Distribution

Ask BIG

AN APPIETITE FOR MORE

Prayer JOURNAL

DR. YVONNE CAPEHART

PUBLISHING COMPANY

THIS JOURNAL BELONGS TO

Ask BIG

"The LORD is my shepherd; I shall not want.
He maketh me to lie down in green pastures:
he leadeth me beside the still waters.
He restoreth my soul: he leadeth me in the
paths of righteousness for his name's sake.
Yea, though I walk through the valley of the
shadow of death, I will fear no evil: for thou
art with me; thy rod and thy staff they
comfort me. Thou preparest a table before
me in the presence of mine enemies: thou
anointest my head with oil; my cup runneth
over. Surely goodness and mercy shall follow
me all the days of my life: and I will dwell in
the house of the LORD for ever."

Psalm 23

Can you imagine receiving everything that you have asked God for and more? Can you imagine yourself no longer living in lack? Can you imagine yourself living as the head and not the tail, above and not beneath?

Allow the imaginations of your heart to began to verbally express the desires of your heart. God, our Master Chef, has invited you to be seated at His banquet table. He is listening, waiting, and ready to create a divine master piece prepared just for you. His simple question for you today is, "What do you have a desire for?"

Ask yourself what is it that you really want in life. Why are you afraid to ask God for it?

ASK BIG is the perfect prayer journal to quince your appetite of faith to cause you to be bold enough to go beyond the boundaries of your fear an leap into a limitless season of faith to receive whatsoever you ask for. Not only ask for it, but ASK BIG.

"Ask, and it will be given to you; seek, and you will find; knock, and it will be opened to you."

Matthew 7:7

JOURNAL INSTRUCTIONS

The ASK BIG 21 day Prayer Journal is a three part journal:

1) **Daily Prayer**: Meditate on your favorite scripture.

2) **Daily Plate**: A) Each day as you are asking God to fill your plate, What are the things you are expecting to happen First?

    A) **Appetizers:** What are you expecting now?

    B) **The Entrée :** What are you expecting in the future?

    C) **The Dessert:** What are the extra desires that you are expecting above your dreams.

3) **Daily Note:** Write your daily notes of the things you were bold enough to believe for and to ASK BIG for.

DATE:

PRAYER	NOTES

Daily Plate

BOLD ENOUGH TO WANT MORE

DATE

Ask **BIG**

APPETIZER

ENTREE

DESSERT

Daily Manna
HUNGRY ENOUGH TO WANT MORE

DATE

SCRIPTURE:

OBSERVATION:

APPLICATION:

PRAYER:

Daily Notes

"And I will do whatever you ask in my name, so that the Father may be glorified in the Son."
John 14:13

DATE:

EMPOWERMENT SCRIPTURE

"The Lord will command the blessing on you in your barns and in all that you undertake. And he will bless you in the land that the Lord your God is giving you." **Deuteronomy 28:8**

PRAYER	NOTES

Daily Plate
BOLD ENOUGH TO WANT MORE

DATE

Ask BIG

APPETIZER

ENTREE

DESSERT

HUNGRY ENOUGH TO WANT MORE

DATE

SCRIPTURE:

OBSERVATION:

APPLICATION:

PRAYER:

Daily Notes

"Jabez cried out to the God of Israel, saying, "Oh that You would indeed bless me and enlarge my border [property], and that Your hand would be with me, and You would keep me from evil so that it does not hurt me!" And God granted his request."

1 Chronicles 4:10

Ask BIG

DATE:

PRAYER	NOTES

24

BOLD ENOUGH TO WANT MORE

DATE

Ask **BIG**

APPETIZER

ENTREE

DESSERT

THIRSTY ENOUGH TO WANT MORE

DATE

SCRIPTURE:

OBSERVATION:

APPLICATION:

PRAYER:

Daily Notes

"Blessed *are* they which do hunger and thirst after righteousness: for they shall be filled."
Matthew 5:6

DATE:

PRAYER	NOTES

BOLD ENOUGH TO WANT MORE

Ask BIG

APPETIZER

ENTREE

DESSERT

THIRSTY ENOUGH TO WANT MORE

DATE

SCRIPTURE:

OBSERVATION:

APPLICATION:

PRAYER:

Daily Notes

"…… Ye have not because
ye ask not."
James 4:2

Ask BIG

DATE:

"And I will make of you a great nation, and I will bless you and make your name great, so that you will be a blessing."
Genesis 12:2

PRAYER	NOTES

BOLD ENOUGH TO WANT MORE

DATE

Ask **BIG**

APPETIZER

ENTREE

DESSERT

Daily Manna
HUNGRY ENOUGH TO WANT MORE

DATE

SCRIPTURE:

OBSERVATION:

APPLICATION:

PRAYER:

Daily Notes

"Blessed are you who hunger now, for you shall be satisfied. Blessed are you who weep now, for you shall laugh,."
Luke 6:21

DATE:

"Blessed is the man who remains steadfast under trial, for when he has stood the test he will receive the crown of life, which God has promised to those who love him." **James 1:12**

PRAYER	NOTES

42

Daily Plate
BOLD ENOUGH TO WANT MORE

DATE

Ask BIG

APPETIZER

ENTREE

DESSERT

Daily Manna
THIRSTY ENOUGH TO WANT MORE

DATE

SCRIPTURE:

OBSERVATION:

APPLICATION:

PRAYER:

Daily Notes

"Now to the *One* being able to do exceedingly above all things that we ask or think, according to the power working in us,."
Ephesians 3:20

DATE:

"Blessed is the man who remains steadfast under trial, for when he has stood the test he will receive the crown of life, which God has promised to those who love him." **James 1:12**

PRAYER	NOTES

48

BOLD ENOUGH TO WANT MORE

DATE

Ask **BIG**

APPETIZER

ENTREE

DESSERT

THIRSTY ENOUGH TO WANT MORE

DATE

SCRIPTURE:

OBSERVATION:

APPLICATION:

PRAYER:

Daily Notes

"Beloved, I wish above all things that thou mayest prosper and be in health. Even as thy soul prospereth."
3 JOHN 2

DATE:

EMPOWERMENT SCRIPTURE

"For I know the plans I have for you, declares the Lord, plans for welfare and not for evil, to give you a future and a hope."
Jeremiah 29:11

PRAYER	NOTES

Daily Plate
BOLD ENOUGH TO WANT MORE

DATE

Ask **BIG**

APPETIZER

ENTREE

DESSERT

55

Daily Manna
HUNGRY ENOUGH TO WANT MORE

DATE

SCRIPTURE:

OBSERVATION:

APPLICATION:

PRAYER:

Daily Notes

"For the LORD God *is* a sun and shield: the LORD will give grace and glory: no good *thing* will he withhold from them that walk uprightly.
Psalm 84:11

DATE:

"You shall eat in plenty and be satisfied, and praise the name of the Lord your God, who has dealt wondrously with you. And my people shall never again be put to shame ." **Joel 2:26**

PRAYER	NOTES

BOLD ENOUGH TO WANT MORE

DATE

Ask **BIG**

APPETIZER

ENTREE

DESSERT

THIRSTY ENOUGH TO WANT MORE

DATE

SCRIPTURE:

OBSERVATION:

APPLICATION:

PRAYER:

Daily Notes

"But my God shall supply all your need according to his riches in glory by Christ Jesus."
Philippians 4:19

DATE:

"The blessing of the Lord makes rich, and he adds no sorrow with it.." **Proverbs 10:22**

PRAYER	NOTES

BOLD ENOUGH TO WANT MORE

Ask BIG

APPETIZER

ENTREE

DESSERT

HUNGRY ENOUGH TO WANT MORE

DATE

SCRIPTURE:

OBSERVATION:

APPLICATION:

PRAYER:

Daily Notes

"....Elijah said unto Elisha, Ask what I shall do for thee, before I be taken away from thee. And Elisha said, I pray thee, let a double portion of thy spirit be upon me.."
2 Kings 2:9

DATE:

PRAYER	NOTES

Daily Plate

BOLD ENOUGH TO WANT MORE

DATE

Ask BIG

APPETIZER

ENTREE

DESSERT

THIRSTY ENOUGH TO WANT MORE

DATE

SCRIPTURE:

OBSERVATION:

APPLICATION:

PRAYER:

Daily Notes

"Please, O LORD, remember how I have walked before You faithfully and with wholehearted devotion; I have done what was good in Your sight."
2 Kings 20:3

DATE:

"Now faith is the assurance of things hoped for, the conviction of things not seen." **Hebrew 11:1**

PRAYER	NOTES

78

BOLD ENOUGH TO WANT MORE

DATE

Ask **BIG**

APPETIZER

ENTREE

DESSERT

HUNGRY ENOUGH TO WANT MORE

DATE

SCRIPTURE:

OBSERVATION:

APPLICATION:

PRAYER:

Daily Notes

"If ye be willing and
obedient, ye shall eat the
good of the land."
Isaiah 1:19

DATE:

"For we walk by faith, not by sight." **2 Corinthians 5:7**

PRAYER	NOTES

Daily Plate

BOLD ENOUGH TO WANT MORE

DATE

Ask **BIG**

APPETIZER

ENTREE

DESSERT

THIRSTY ENOUGH TO WANT MORE

DATE

SCRIPTURE:

OBSERVATION:

APPLICATION:

PRAYER:

Daily Notes

Ask **BIG**

"As the deer pants for the water brooks, So my soul pants for Thee, O God."
Psalm 42:1

DATE:

"For nothing will be impossible with God."." **Luke 1:37**

PRAYER	NOTES

Daily Plate
BOLD ENOUGH TO WANT MORE

DATE

Ask BIG

APPETIZER

ENTREE

DESSERT

HUNGRY ENOUGH TO WANT MORE

DATE

SCRIPTURE:

OBSERVATION:

APPLICATION:

PRAYER:

Daily Notes

Ask **BIG**

"Therefore I say unto you,
What things soever ye
desire, when ye pray,
believe that ye
receive *them*, and ye shall
have *them*."
Mark 11:24

DATE:

"The apostles said to the Lord, "Increase our faith!."
Luke 17:5

PRAYER	NOTES

Daily Plate
BOLD ENOUGH TO WANT MORE

DATE

Ask BIG

APPETIZER

ENTREE

DESSERT

Daily Manna
THIRSTY ENOUGH TO WANT MORE

DATE

SCRIPTURE:

OBSERVATION:

APPLICATION:

PRAYER:

Daily Notes

"When you have eaten
and are satisfied, you shall
bless the Lord your God
for the good land which
He has given."
Deuteronomy 8:10

DATE:

EMPOWERMENT SCRIPTURE

"And Jesus said to him, "If you can! All things are possible for one who believes!." **Mark 9:3**

PRAYER	NOTES

Daily Plate

BOLD ENOUGH TO WANT MORE

DATE

Ask **BIG**

APPETIZER

ENTREE

DESSERT

HUNGRY ENOUGH TO WANT MORE

DATE

SCRIPTURE:

OBSERVATION:

APPLICATION:

PRAYER:

Daily Notes

"Be careful for nothing; but in every thing by prayer and supplication with thanksgiving let your requests be made known unto God."
Philippians 4:6

DATE:

EMPOWERMENT SCRIPTURE

"I can do all things through him who strengthens me."
Philippians 4:13

PRAYER	NOTES

BOLD ENOUGH TO WANT MORE

Ask BIG

APPETIZER

ENTREE

DESSERT

THIRSTY ENOUGH TO WANT MORE

SCRIPTURE:

OBSERVATION:

APPLICATION:

PRAYER:

Daily Notes

"If ye abide in me, and my words abide in you, ye shall ask what ye will, and it shall be done unto you."
John 15:7

DATE:

"May he give you the desire of your heart and make all your plans succeed." **Psalm 20:4**

PRAYER	NOTES

BOLD ENOUGH TO WANT MORE

DATE

Ask BIG

APPETIZER

ENTREE

DESSERT

115

HUNGRY ENOUGH TO WANT MORE

DATE

SCRIPTURE:

OBSERVATION:

APPLICATION:

PRAYER:

Daily Notes

"Therefore I say unto you, What things soever ye desire, when ye pray, believe that ye receive them, and ye shall have them."
Mark 11:24

DATE:

"Worship the Lord your God, and his blessing will be on your food and water. I will take away sickness from among you." **Exodus 23:25**

PRAYER	NOTES

BOLD ENOUGH TO WANT MORE

Ask BIG

APPETIZER

ENTREE

DESSERT

THIRSTY ENOUGH TO WANT MORE

DATE

SCRIPTURE:

OBSERVATION:

APPLICATION:

PRAYER:

Daily Notes

"Delight thyself also in the LORD; and he shall give thee the desires of thine hear."
Psalms 37:4

DATE:

"Whoever gives heed to instruction prospers, and blessed is the one who trusts in the Lord."   **Proverbs 16:20**

PRAYER	NOTES

BOLD ENOUGH TO WANT MORE

DATE

Ask BIG

APPETIZER	ENTREE

DESSERT

Daily Manna
HUNGRY ENOUGH TO WANT MORE

DATE

SCRIPTURE:

OBSERVATION:

APPLICATION:

PRAYER:

Daily Notes

"And whatever we ask we receive from him, because we keep his commandments and do what pleases him."
1 John 3:22

Ask BIG

DATE:

PRAYER	NOTES

Daily Plate
BOLD ENOUGH TO WANT MORE

DATE

Ask**BIG**

APPETIZER

ENTREE

DESSERT

THIRSTY ENOUGH TO WANT MORE

DATE

SCRIPTURE:

OBSERVATION:

APPLICATION:

PRAYER:

Daily Notes

If you have enjoyed
ASK BIG, 21day journal prepare now
to quench your appetite even more
with "BE SEATED PLEASE: From the
Battle to the Banquet." along with the
ASK BIG DESTINY TOOL KIT

BE SEATED PLEASE
BOOK
13- 978-0-9710441-6-6

ASK BIG
DESTINY TOOL KIT
13- 979-8-9858337-0-6

www.askbingonline.com
www.yvonnecapehart.org

Made in the USA
Columbia, SC
10 July 2023

20158109R00076